How to paint on GLASS

*To my husband, Paul, for all his help and support,
and to my parents, for all their encouragement.*

How to paint on
GLASS

Julia Bottrell

SEARCH PRESS

First published in Great Britain 1996

Search Press Limited
Wellwood, North Farm Road,
Tunbridge Wells, Kent TN2 3DR

There are references to sable brushes in this book. It is the
Publishers' custom to recommend synthetic materials as
substitutes for animal products wherever possible: many
brushes made from artificial fibres will be found to be as
satisfactory as brushes made of natural fibres.

If you have difficulty in obtaining any of the materials or
equipment mentioned in this book, please write for further
information to the Publishers.
Search Press Limited, Wellwood, North Farm Road,
Tunbridge Wells, Kent TN2 3DR, England.

*Page 1: This picture of a hen was painted on a 180 x
165mm (7 x 6¹/₂in) sheet of acetate for an Easter card. The
design could also be used for a suncatcher in a kitchen.*

Page 2–3: Gothic candle-shade (see pages 24–25).

*Page 4–5: Paint a butterfly on thin acetate, cut it to shape,
fold it in half and wrap a coloured pipe cleaner around the
middle for the body. You can then attach it anywhere for
instant decoration (see page 80).*

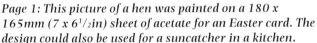

ISBN 0 85532 809 6

Printed in Spain by Elkar S. Coop, 48012 Bilbao

Contents

A collection of three-dimensional objects transformed with glass paints. It includes a purchased glass box, two recycled coffee jars, a purchased glass vase and an old terrarium which had a couple of cracked panes of glass. Instructions for painting three-dimensional objects will be found on pages 18–19.

Introduction

If you have ever wished you could make your own stained glass, but never tried because you thought it was too difficult, this book is for you. I am going to show you the easy way of making beautiful 'stained-glass' images, using a simple new technique.

People have been making stained glass for a very long time. Even the ancient Romans used it in their temples. During the Middle Ages, when the great cathedrals of Europe were built, enormous stained-glass windows were constructed, illustrating scenes from the Bible for the largely illiterate congregations of the time.

Stained glass has continued to be made from then up to the present day. Although the subject-matter of the designs has diversified, there is one thing that all these works, both old and new, have in common; one thing that has not changed a great deal in all that time – the basic method of construction. Now, as then, this involves the slow and difficult process of cutting lead, selecting coloured glass, cutting this to size and then assembling all these components to form an image. Details such as faces and lettering are actually painted, and are then fired.

The results are very beautiful, but, not surprisingly, people find the skills and craftsmanship required for traditional stained glass off-putting.

Now, thanks to new materials and a totally different approach, you can create the *appearance* of stained glass on a single piece of glass or plastic. Liquid 'lead' and transparent paints, which are readily available from craft shops, are drawn and painted on to the surface of glass or plastic, enabling you to create beautiful stained-glass effects quickly and easily on virtually anything transparent. The method is so simple that a child can do it. A project can be completed from start to finish in a matter of hours instead of the days it would take using the traditional method.

The easy techniques you will need are all in this book. With a bit of practice, it will not be long before you start painting your own family heirlooms!

See page 64 for the pattern.

Materials and equipment

On the following pages I tell you about the materials and tools used for painting on glass (the numbers refer to the photograph on pages 10–11). Glass painting is a craft that you can grow into. To start with you need just a few colours, a tube of leading and a sheet of plastic.

Transparent surfaces to paint on

Glass (4) is cheap and durable, it does not scratch easily and it can be cut to size when you buy it. Ask your glazier to smooth the edges of the glass to make it safer to handle. If you want to fix a glass painting to an existing window (see page 63), paint on lightweight picture glass. You can also buy ready-made glass 'suncatcher' shapes (5) and leaded boxes (19) from craft shops or you might like to recycle old jam jars (3) and bottles.

Although more expensive, sheets of clear plastic are much lighter in weight than glass, and, as they do not shatter when dropped, they are better for children to use. To make the shrink-plastic projects on page 56 you will need to buy a special plastic – this is also readily available from craft shops.

Thin sheets of acetate are easily cut with scissors and are very good for making your own shapes (see the butterflies on pages 4–5). You can also use them to make inserts for greetings cards (see page 17) and candle-shades (pages 22–25).

It is a good idea to keep scraps of plastic and acetate to practise your painting on.

Leading

Liquid lead (22) is a thick, non-toxic, acrylic-based paste which comes in tubes or large bottles – generally in four shades (black, silver, gold and imitation lead). It is squeezed straight from its tube via an attached nozzle which makes it easy to control the flow and thickness of the line.

Fix a gutta nib (21) – a round metal nib used for painting on silk – on the end of the nozzle to make fine leading for smaller pieces of work. I suggest using a No. 9 size. Nibs must be thoroughly cleaned immediately after use, as they do tend to clog up.

You can also buy a special peel-off leading (23) which, although intended for use with textured paints, can be used with other types of paint.

For a more realistic look to your painting you can use self-adhesive lead strip (20) which comes complete with a pressing tool (16). I show you how to use this on pages 28 and 48–51.

Paints

Transparent paints (1) are made especially for stained-glass painting. There are also white and black paints, which are opaque.

You can buy either water-based (acrylic) or solvent-based paints. Both solvent-based and acrylic paints can be painted over with extra layers of paint when dry, but the two types of paint cannot be mixed with each other. Both types give an excellent finish.

Water-based paints have a rather limited colour range, but they are easy to use; water is used to thin the paint and to clean the brushes.

If you would like a lighter, more transparent colour without thinning the texture of water-based paint, you can use a colourless acrylic medium.

Water-based textured paints (18) are applied straight from the tube or bottle and are very good for making temporary window decorations (see pages 44–47).

Solvent-based paints are durable and have an extensive colour range. They are also much less likely to fade in direct sunlight than the water-based acrylic paint, but may have a strong odour. Use varnish to create a more transparent colour. Only solvent-based paints are suitable for the vat-dipping method (see page 58).

These paints are thinned with white spirit (7), which must also be used to clean the brushes.

Some manufacturers of glass-painting materials make their own brands of thinners and brush cleaners. However, I find it much more economical, and just as effective, to buy the large plastic containers of white spirit, which are readily available from DIY stores.

Palettes and brushes

It is important to be able to keep colours separate from each other, so you will need a plastic palette (9) with several deep wells.

When using glass paints, it is essential to use brushes that can carry paint smoothly, leaving no 'tracks' on the surface. Some craft suppliers stock 'round ceramic' brushes, which they say are specifically designed for use with transparent and ceramic paints, but I always use a fine-point ox/sable or white nylon No. 4 brush. The fineness of the brush tip makes it easy to reach into any awkward areas of leaded work.

For larger areas, use a No. 8 or No. 10 brush. If you are adding fine lines of detail to a dry area that has already been painted, use a No. 1 brush.

Sticky tape and double-sided tape

Use sticky tape (10) to anchor your work in place and stop it moving about while you are leading and painting. Use double-sided tape (14) for fastening together the edges of candle shades. This is also useful for securing templates to glass and plastic when painting to the very edge of an object.

Varnishes

Special varnish (8) for protecting stained-glass paint can be used to protect your finished work if it is going to be cleaned regularly or if it is likely to be knocked or scuffed (see the sealing, care and cleaning tips on page 62).

There is also a special material called frosting varnish (24) which gives the effect of acid etching (see page 52).

Other accessories

Cotton buds (26) and tissues (27) are useful for removing paint that has accidentally run or been spilt on your painting. Your craft kit could also include a scalpel (17), a pair of scissors (15), a pencil and eraser (11), a china-marking crayon, some strong glue (13), some cocktail sticks (28), tracing and plain white paper (6), nylon thread (12) and cord (25) for hanging mobiles, etc., and some blank greetings cards (2).

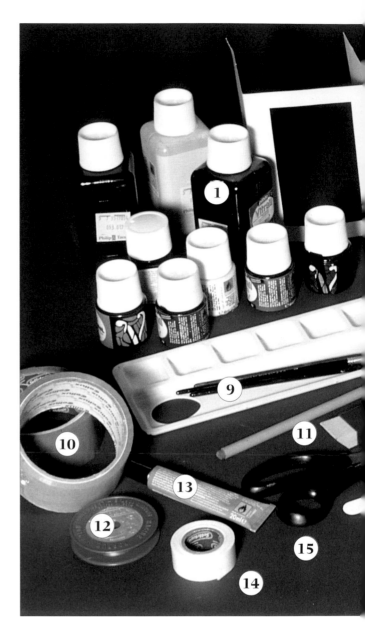

Glass-painting easel

When painting panels, the glass or plastic sheet would ordinarily be held in place with tape to stop it moving around while you work. The glass-painting easel (opposite), which is available by mail order, will hold panels firmly while you work, either horizontally or vertically. It has a movable bar to support your hand while you work, protecting your painting from accidental smudging. You can also move your work, if you need to, easily and safely, while it is held firmly in the easel.

Ventilation

Make sure that the room in which you will be painting is adequately ventilated. Leave windows open or, if you have one, use an extractor fan. This is important if you are working with solvent-based paints as it will help avoid headaches from the smell of paint and white spirit! If possible, work outside on a dry warm day, as this will also speed up the drying times.

The basic method

Drawing and tracing the pattern (1)

Work on a large flat surface and protect it with newspapers. Prepare the liquid lead by piercing the nozzle with a long pin or needle and keep it handy. If you want thinner lines, fit a nib on the nozzle (see page 9).

Trace the design using a black pen, back it with a sheet of white paper and then secure both beneath a clean sheet of glass or acetate with masking tape.

Applying the liquid lead (2)

With a steady hand, apply even pressure on the tube, lightly rest the tip of the nozzle on the surface of the acetate, and draw the lead across the surface. You get thick lines by applying more pressure and moving slowly across the surface; thin lines by applying less pressure and moving more quickly.

Trace individual lines of the template. After each line, stop and wipe the nozzle with a tissue as it can easily become clogged with lead.

Checking the outlines (3)

When the lead outlines are complete, unfasten three sides of the template and, taking care not to smudge it, hold the image up to the light and look for any gaps and errors. Correct small errors by wiping off wet lead with a damp cotton bud. If the lead has dried, pick off small areas with your fingernail. When you are happy with the result, leave it to dry. Depending on the thickness of the lines, this should take between 30 minutes and 3 hours.

Starting to apply colour (4)

As you can see, the lead lines stand proud of the surface and create separate areas within the design. Fill these in with paint, and the lead will hold each colour separate, giving the appearance of individual pieces of coloured glass.

Start by carefully applying paint around the inside edge of the leaded area. This will ensure that all corners are filled with paint, avoiding any tiny missed bits!

Filling in colour (5)

Now, making sure the brush is really loaded with paint, fill in the centre of the area to ensure an even colour. The paint should be diluted enough that it almost drips from the brush. Continue painting each area in the colours of your choice. Paint one colour at a time, cleaning the brush thoroughly between colour changes.

Correcting mistakes (6)

Any mistakes can be cleaned off immediately while still wet using a cotton bud.

Tips

◆ Always squeeze the tube from the bottom to avoid uneven lines and 'sputtering' when air gets into the tube. Always replace the cap on the tube. Wash nibs thoroughly.

◆ I am left-handed, so I always start painting from the top right-hand corner and work across and down the image to avoid smudging. If you are right-handed start at the top left-hand corner.

◆ Decant colours and mix them in a palette or saucer. Dilute solvent paints with a few drops of white spirit, and water-based paints with water.

◆ Never mix water-based paints with solvent paints. Mix your own colours by using one or the other.

◆ Accelerate the drying time of liquid lead by using a hair dryer on a low setting.

Drying

Now leave your work on a flat surface to dry for approximately eight hours. When it is dry, hold it up to the light to see if you have missed any small areas, for example, in the corners. If you have, dab a little of the liquid lead into the corner to cover it; this is less noticeable than adding little dabs of paint.

The finished picture.

Projects

In this chapter I have included a variety of projects for you to try; cards, mobiles, candle-shades, jars, bottles, baubles and boxes, and a couple of panels.

I start with the simplest of projects – a greetings card . . . small, flat and unbreakable . . . just a small piece of acetate is all you need to paint on. Craft shops sell thin acetate by the sheet, but lots of throw-away packaging is made of acetate and this can be just as easily cut and painted.

Iris card

You will need

80 x 130mm (3^1/$_4$ x 5^1/$_4$in) piece of acetate

Tube of black lead

Gutta nib

Tracing paper and white paper

Blank aperture card 110 x 150mm (4^1/$_4$ x 6in) with a 70 x 120mm (2^3/$_4$ x 4^3/$_4$in) aperture

Sticky tape

Tissues and cotton buds

No. 3 ox-hair/sable brush

Solvent-based paints: purple, white, yellow and emerald green

Thinners

Sunflower card

You will need

All the items listed for the iris card (except for the black leading and paints) plus:

Tube of gold lead

Paints: brown, yellow, orange and green

When using gold or silver lead for outlining instead of black, be careful not to get any paint on the gold lead, as it stains easily. If any paint does go over the lead, wipe it off quickly with a cotton bud dipped in thinners (or water for water-based paint). When wet, gold lead appears light in colour, but it dries to a richer, darker tone.

If you do stain the lead, you can turn the painting over and show the reverse side instead, as I have done in the example shown below. It will look neater but the leading will not have the raised effect.

1. Trace the design and complete the leading in black (see pages 12–13). Lift the acetate to see if any lines have been missed, then carefully place it back into position and leave it to dry.

2. When the lead has dried, paint the centre of the flower in white and yellow. The white paint will remain opaque. Make sure that the paint has been sufficiently thinned so that you can paint right into awkward shapes and corners. Do not worry if the paint goes over the black lead, as this will not stain.

3. Now paint the stem and leaves in emerald green. To obtain the effect of different shades of one colour, apply undiluted emerald paint on one leaf and very diluted paint on another. Leave to dry.

4. Remove the tape and fit the painting into the card blank.

Making your own card blanks

These are easy to make from thin card. Of course, you do not have to use white; you can equally well use coloured card but, if you use a dark shade, you will need to back your painting with white paper.

Sunflower card showing the reverse of the gold leading.

See page 64 for the pattern.

Dragonflies and butterflies storage jar

Plain old jars can look really outstanding when given the 'stained-glass' treatment; so good, in fact, that the jar's humble origins are not immediately apparent. Painting the jar is easy, though it does involve a slight change of method.

Before painting, make sure that the jar is really clean by washing and drying it thoroughly.

You will need

Glass jar
One or two tubes of black liquid lead
Gutta nib
Tracing paper and white paper
Two small weights (to stop the jar rolling about)
Sticky tape
Tissues and cotton buds
No. 3 ox-hair/sable brush
Paints: yellow, orange, green and blue
Thinners

1. Trace or photocopy the templates printed on this page, cut out each design separately, and arrange them around the jar.

2. When you are satisfied with their positions, tape them on the inside of the jar using sticky tape. Roll up a small sheet of white paper into a tube and put this inside the jar. This will create a white background, making the templates easier to see.

3. Lay the jar on its side. Place a small weight on either side of the jar to keep it still while you apply the lead.

4. Now draw the leaded lines around the uppermost template on the outside of the jar.

5. When this has dried, roll the jar around to the next template and draw this with lead. Continue in this way until all the templates have been outlined with lead. Check to make sure you have not missed any of the lines on the templates.

Lay the jar on its side and support it with a couple of weights while you paint the design.

6. Place the jar on its side, supported on either side as before, and prepare your paints. When painting a rounded surface, it is easier to control the flow of paint if it is not diluted too much, so do not use too much thinners.

7. With the jar in place, paint the uppermost design. Leave this part to dry before moving the jar around to the next design. Continue in this way until you have painted all the designs.

8. For extra protection of the work, you can seal the painted area with varnish (see page 62).

The decorated storage jar filled with sugar.

Christmas mobile

This Christmas mobile would make a lovely present, but you may want to keep it for yourself!

For safety reasons, I always recommend using plastic or acetate for mobiles. Acetate is easily cut into shapes, or you could buy pre-cut pieces from a craft shop.

I think it is best to buy the slightly thicker plastic for mobiles, as it tends to hang better. Have it cut into rounds. Also, ask your supplier to make a small hole near the outer edge in each piece for threading.

You will need

Four 130mm (about 5in) diameter roundels of plastic or acetate (three with one hole, and one with two holes opposite each other)

Three to four tubes of black lead

An old wire coat-hanger

A pair of pliers

About 750mm (30in) strong nylon thread

Tracing paper and white paper

Double-sided sticky tape

Tissues and cotton buds

No. 4 ox-hair/sable brush

Paints: blue, yellow, orange, white, brown, purple, white, pink, red, grey, green

Thinners

1. Trace the templates on pages 65–66 and back them with white paper. Position the roundels on top of each template and secure them with pieces of double-sided tape. The templates have to be held in this way because this time you will be applying paint right up to the edges of the roundels.

2. Trace the templates with black lead, making sure that you do not miss any of the lines of the design.

3. When the lead has dried, paint the roundels. Choose your own colours or use the ones in the photograph. Allow the paint to dry while you are constructing the other parts of the mobile.

4. Using pliers, cut a 370mm (14$\frac{1}{2}$in) length of wire from the coat hanger. Bend over each end to form downward-facing loops. Grip the wire with your hands and gently bend it into a slightly bowed shape.

5. Using the picture below as a guide, cut nylon thread into lengths and fasten one roundel to each end of the wire.

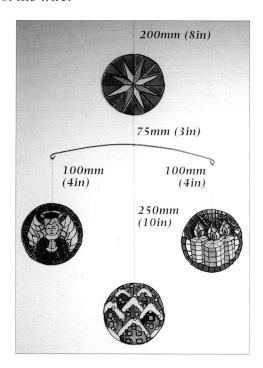

200mm (8in)

75mm (3in)

100mm (4in)   100mm (4in)

250mm (10in)

6. To hang evenly, the central thread, to which the other two roundels are attached, must be tied into position at the exact midpoint of the wire. To prevent a lopsided appearance, rest the wire on your outstretched finger; you will see if you have the balance correct. Adjust the position until you are satisfied, then mark the point with a felt-tipped pen.

7. Tie the bottom roundel on to a length of thread, then wind the thread several times around the mid-point of the hanger. Continue on with the thread and tie it on to the bottom of the last roundel. Tie the remaining thread on to the top of the roundel.

To hang the mobile, you can attach a metal ring to the top of the thread, or simply tie a loop in the end the thread.

See pages 65–66 for the patterns.

20

Tulip candle-shade

Candle-shades enhance the appearance of any room, and I think that stained-glass candle-shades are the most beautiful of all. All you need to make these lovely atmospheric candle-shades is a sheet of acetate, double-sided tape, glass paint, and, of course, a candle!

Here I have created an Art-Nouveau-inspired tulip design reminiscent of Tiffany lamps.

You will need

A 250 x 320mm (10 x 12¹/₂in) sheet of acetate

Two to three tubes of black lead

Tracing paper and white paper

Tissues and cotton buds

Double-sided sticky tape

Nos. 4 and 8 ox-hair/sable brushes

Paints: blue, red, purple, emerald green, leaf green and olive green

Thinners

1. Copy the design on pages 68–69 on to tracing paper and back this with white paper. Fasten this to your work surface.

2. Using double-sided tape, fasten the acetate on top. (You will be painting the entire sheet, leaving no margins, so this is the best way of keeping the sheet in position.)

3. Trace the design on to the acetate with black lead. Check that all the lines of the design have been traced. Leave to dry.

4. Using a No. 8 brush, paint the upper background in blue. Make sure that the paint is diluted sufficiently so that you can spread it around quickly and evenly. If any of the paint accidentally spreads into flowers or stems, wipe it off with a cotton bud dipped in thinners.

5. Paint the flowers in red and purple, using a No. 4 brush. Make sure that the paint is sufficiently diluted for an even coverage.

6. Paint the stems and leaves with leaf green and emerald green, using a No. 8 brush. Then, while

the paint is still wet, drag a No. 4 brush, using undiluted leaf or emerald green, along the length of each leaf. This will give the leaves added surface texture. Leave the painting to dry.

To make the shade

Keeping the painting side uppermost, attach a strip of double-sided sticky tape down one of the short sides.

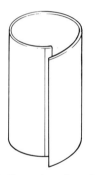

With the painted surface on the outside, curl the acetate sheet around to form a cylinder...

...then press the edges together firmly to form the candle-shade.

Using your acetate candle-shade

Place a small metal-cased night-light (available from supermarkets) into a clear glass jar before placing it into the candle-shade. For safety reasons, the jar should always be taller than the height of the naked flame.

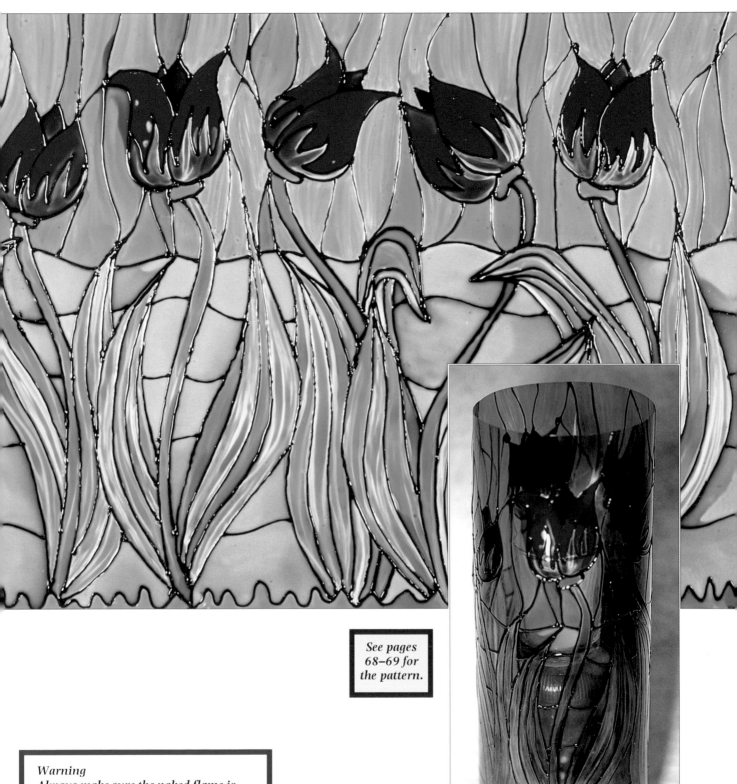

See pages
68–69 for
the pattern.

Warning
Always make sure the naked flame is
protected with a glass jar. If you have a
tall glass, you can use real candles.
This also applies to the shade on the
following pages.

Gothic candle-shade

This rather unusual Gothic candle-shade has its own little stained-glass windows.

You will need
A 250 x 320mm (10 x 12½in) sheet of acetate
Two to three tubes silver lead
Tracing paper and white paper
Tissues and cotton buds
Double-sided sticky tape
No. 4 and 8 ox-hair/sable brushes
Paints: grey, blue, green, red, orange and yellow
Thinners

1. Follow stages 1–3 as for the tulip shade, using silver lead instead of black.

2. Paint the grey background using the 'dappling' technique (see page 55).

3. Paint in the windows, using the colours shown in the photograph as a guide. Remember that silver and gold lead stains easily, so be careful.

4. When it is dry, you may wish to cut away the unpainted area at the top of the shade to make an interesting shaped edge. Assemble the candle-shade together as shown on page 22.

The completed candle-shade – the photograph at the left shows how it appears in natural daylight; the one below shows the effect created by candlelight alone.

See page 67 for the pattern.

Suncatchers

Suncatchers look very bright and cheerful when hung against a window – even the simplest design can look really attractive.

A glazier will cut shapes for you, but ready-cut pieces, complete with holes for hanging, are available from craft shops or by mail order. These come in all shapes and sizes – from small hearts to large circles.

Suncatchers are quick and easy to paint; just follow the instructions for the basic method on pages 12–14. They can be painted and hung just as they are, with plain edges, or you can seal the edges with self-adhesive lead (see page 28).

Temporary, stick-on suncatchers can also be made using peel-off leading and paint (see pages 46–47).

A suncatcher looks very pretty in a bedroom when hung in a window by a brightly coloured ribbon. This one has been finished off with self-adhesive lead round the edges.

See page 70 for the pattern.

This robin has been painted in a less stylised fashion than many of my other glass paintings. There is no pattern for the robin.

*A free-flowing style
using opaque black
paint and a minimum
of leaded lines.*

Self-adhesive-lead edges

For a free-hanging suncatcher, you can apply self-adhesive lead around the edge to give a neat finish.

Then you can attach a metal clip and a chain (available from craft shops or by mail order) and hang your suncatcher on a window. You can also buy ready-to-hang lead-framed suncatchers with plain glass.

An alternative is to attach the clip to a transparent plastic 'sucker' which fastens on to the window, but these will not take too much weight, so only use them with small suncatchers.

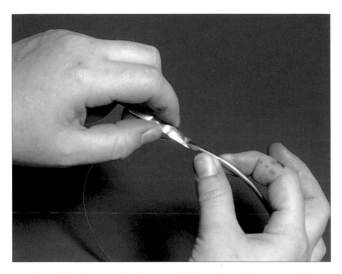

Apply self-adhesive lead around the edge of the roundel.

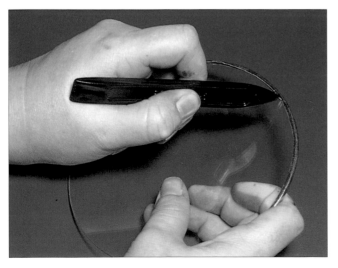

Ensure the lead strip is well stuck down by burnishing it with the pressing tool provided with the leading kit. You could also use a bone folder or a spoon.

Fixing suncatchers in windows

Suncatchers of all shapes can be fixed to existing windows with wide self-adhesive lead using the method shown on page 63. For a roundel, measure its circumference and cut the leading to size. Temporarily, secure the roundel in position with a piece of masking tape at the top; this will make it easier for you to apply the lead.

Starting at the bottom of the circle, press the lead around the edge, with half of its width on the suncatcher, and half on the window. Continue in this way until you reach the place where you started. Overlap the lead by about 10mm ($^3/_8$in), sealing the join firmly.

See page 70 for the pattern.

This lighthouse suncatcher, painted on a pre-leaded sheet of glass, would look striking hung against a bathroom window.

Glass panel dragon

This striking dragon is made using the basic method on pages 12–14, yet it looks very impressive.

Any glass painting can be permanently fixed on to an existing sheet of glass, but the painting must be on lightweight picture glass so that it is easy to handle and not too heavy. Another advantage is that thin glass will not stand too proud of the surface of the existing glass beneath, making it much easier to fix into place. Any glazier will supply you with picture glass. For safety reasons, I recommend that the dimensions of the picture glass do not exceed 400 x 300mm (16 x 12in).

If you are fixing a glass painting into a wooden frame, there is no need to use lightweight picture glass. The painting is placed into the frame and held in place with strips of wooden beading nailed into place to keep the glass secure. For more details on fixing glass, see page 63.

You will need

A sheet of picture glass
Three to four tubes of black lead
Tracing paper and white paper
Tissues and cotton buds
Sticky tape
No. 4 ox-hair/sable brush
Varnish and No. 8 brush
Paints: emerald green, leaf green, yellow, black, red, white
Thinners
Optional: textured clear paint

1. Trace the design with lead, as before.

2. Paint the dragon, using the photograph as a guide to the colours.

3. When it is completely dry, varnish the whole panel, including the clear leaded background, using a No. 8 brush (see note below).

Note: This example includes the optional textured clear paint (I tell you more about this on page 47). It is water-based so, if you want to seal the solvent-based paints with varnish, be very careful not to get any varnish on the background.

See pages 72–73 for the pattern.

30

Image size: 340 x 220mm (13$\frac{1}{2}$ x 8$\frac{3}{4}$in), on glass.

Image size:
250 x 260mm
(9⁷/₈ x 10¹/₄in),
on glass.

**See page 71
for the
pattern.**

Jungle parrot

White is an *opaque* glass paint. When it is mixed with the other colours it produces pleasing pastels which, I think, look very effective used here against the lush background of foliage. Remember to paint your picture on lightweight picture glass if you are planning to fix your completed painting to an existing window. Instructions for fixing are shown on page 63.

You will need

A sheet of picture glass no larger than 400 x 300mm
  (16 x 12in)
Three to four tubes of black lead
Tracing paper and white paper
Sticky tape
Tissues and cotton buds
Nos. 4 and 8 ox-hair/sable brushes
Varnish
Paints: yellow, orange, emerald green, olive green,
  brown, turquoise, pink, white, red and purple
Thinners

1. Trace the template with lead as before.

2. Paint the parrot using mixed combinations of pink, white, red and purple. Use your own colour scheme or use the photograph as a colour guide.

  Try experimenting by mixing white with drops of colour to achieve the shades you require.

3. Paint the sun with yellow and orange, then the foliage with emerald and olive green. As with the tulip candle-shade on pages 22–23, try dragging undiluted colour through the lengths of the leaves.

4. When the panel is completely dry, seal it with varnish to protect it.

Painting on bottles

Coloured bottles

Old wine and spirit bottles are often made of deep, rich shades of green and blue. Instead of throwing them away, why not decorate them using gold or silver lead? Both will produce beautiful contrasting effects on dark bottles.

As bottle necks are too narrow to allow you to place templates on the insides, you must draw your design freehand on the outside, using a light-coloured china-marking crayon. You can then follow these lines with gold or silver lead. Bottles decorated in this way will only stand light washing, and must be used for decorative purposes only. You can, however, make the leading a little stronger by varnishing.

Clear bottles

If you wish to apply both lead and paint, you need to use transparent or light-coloured bottles for the designs to be seen properly. Again, as with all bottles, you will have to draw your designs on the outside using a china-marking crayon. To paint your bottle, follow steps 3–8 for painting a jar (see pages 18–19). Painted bottles can look very appealing, and even an old milk bottle would make a pretty vase when deco-rated in this way.

Painting on boxes

Every Christmas and Easter I am given chocolates in plastic boxes. I think the boxes are far too nice to throw away when empty. Everyone must have at least one of these boxes at home, wondering what would be the best use for it!

By painting a box with the Clarice-Cliffe-inspired design shown here, I think I have found the perfect solution: they make lovely trinket boxes. I painted one for a friend of mine, and she did not even realise that it was the same chocolate box that she had given me for my birthday the previous year!

You will need

A transparent plastic box
Two to three tubes black lead
Tracing paper and white paper
Sticky tape
Tissues and cotton buds
No. 3 ox-hair / sable brush
Paints: yellow, orange, red, purple, white, blue and brown
Thinners

See page 74 for the patterns.

Boxes are easier to paint than jam jars, but they are still three-dimensional shapes, and so have to be painted in stages.

1. Trace the templates on page 74 for each of the box sides and back them with white paper.

2. Secure the templates to the inside surfaces of the box and the lid with sticky tape.

3. Lay the box down on one of its sides. Using lead, draw the design on the surface of the side panel. Turn the box on to its end and trace the template on to the surface of the end panel. Leave these two sides to dry.

4. Repeat the process on the remaining side and end panels, and then the lid. Leave to dry.

5. Place the box on its side and paint one side at a time, using the photograph as a guide. Make sure each panel has dried before turning the box over to paint the next. I like to dilute the paint liberally for this particular design, as a more translucent look gives the box a light and delicate appearance.

6. When completely dry, add a coat of varnish for protection against knocks and scratches.

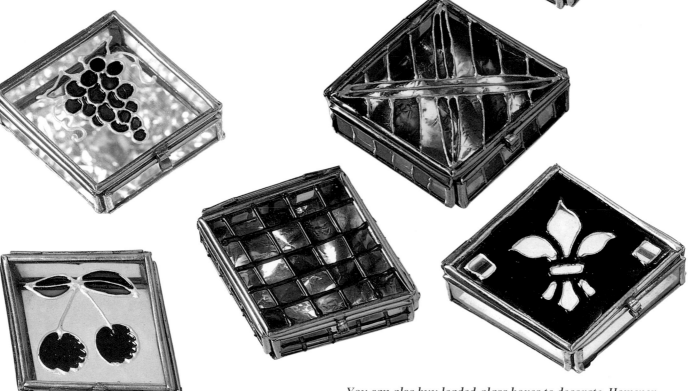

You can also buy leaded-glass boxes to decorate. However, these are usually quite small, so, generally, you can only use the simplest of designs on them.

Baubles

You can now buy transparent three-dimensional glass or acrylic shapes. These look good hanging from windows or room lights, but they also make marvellous Christmas decorations. The most versatile is the globe-shaped variety, as it is easier to paint and offers more scope for design.

I like to decorate them using gold or silver lead; but the darker leads can also look very effective. Then, as they are only subject to light use, I paint them using textured paint (see page 44). This paint can be applied vertically, and straight from its bottle. Children love painting these decorations and, as no brushes or water are needed, they do not make much mess!

Making your own designs

In this book, I have included many outline designs for you to use, but it is also fun to design your own patterns and artwork.

Inspiration

If you would like to produce a traditional piece of work, old cathedrals and churches always have good examples to inspire you. There are, however, many other styles which can be adapted very successfully for glass painting. Art Deco and Art Nouveau, for example, feature interesting images with strong lines that make them very suitable for leaded-glass work.

For images of animals or flowers, try looking in your local library and trace pictures from books. You may even be able to photocopy any pictures that may be of use. Stencils, rubber stamps, embroidery transfers and silk-painting designs are other good sources of inspiration.

Simplicity

Whichever design you choose, the secret is to keep it simple! Not only are strong, simple lines easier to draw with liquid lead, but you will also find that they give your painting a bolder, more authentic stained-glass appearance.

Stylising your design and spacing the lead outlines

1. Here is a photograph that I found on the cover of a diary. Study the picture and determine how you can stylise or simplify it so that it can be transposed on to glass.

2. Now make a tracing from the photograph. The outlines of the image must be solid and unbroken to ensure that each colour you apply will stay in its respective area (within the leaded lines), to give an authentic appearance of separate pieces of coloured glass.

3. Finally, add more lines to break up the background and the larger areas of the petals. You will get a much more even finish to the paintwork when you work in relatively small areas. Extra detail can always be applied later, after the first coat has dried.

Try out different colour schemes with felt-tipped pens before you start painting.

Reducing or enlarging patterns

If your design is too large or small for your purposes, use a photocopier to reduce or enlarge your image to size. If several images are the wrong size, you can photocopy them individually and then place them in position. Additional lines can be added to your template by hand.

If you do not have access to a photocopier, you can reduce or enlarge your patterns using a simple grid system as shown here.

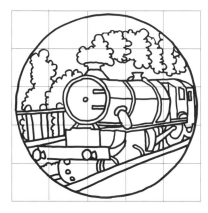

Enlarging a design using the grid method.

Other techniques

See page 75 for the pattern.

Adding jewels and beads

To make your stained-glass work even more interesting, try adding a few jewels or beads. If these are applied while the paint is still wet, no adhesive is required. Simply push the jewel or bead firmly on to the painted surface; when the paint dries, it will be stuck firmly in place. If you intend to embellish an item that has already dried, the jewels and beads can be stuck on with an all-purpose glue.

Adding jewels and beads

◆ Remember to leave sufficient room between leaded lines for the size and shape of the jewels or beads you want to add. It will be extremely difficult to glue over the leaded lines, as these always stand proud of the surface.

◆ It is always better to fix jewels and beads on to the paint *before* it has dried. This is because they can be pressed down into the wet paint, allowing them to be seen clearly on the back of the painting as well as on the front. When applied to a dry area that has been painted, especially if the paint is a dark colour, the jewels and beads may only be visible on the glued side.

*The shape of this bottle inspired me to create an
'Arabian Nights' design. The coloured beads on the
domes and towers give an exotic Eastern touch.*

These two bows, originally made as peel-off suncatchers, now have a new use decorating this mirror.

Using textured paints

See page 76
for the
pattern.

This water-based paint and lead range from America is purely for decoration. It comes in bottles and tubes and is piped directly on to glass or plastic without using brushes – perfect for painting on glass and acrylic Christmas decorations. When dry it can be peeled off the glass and replaced elsewhere. Its non-drip characteristic means that it can be applied to both horizontal and vertical surfaces, which makes it possible to paint an existing door or window *in situ*. However, it must not be used on external windows as it will not tolerate temperature changes, and will become brittle and crack. Also, you should not apply it to internal windows and doors where there is excess moisture, for example kitchens or bathrooms. If moisture condenses on it, the colours may run and stain your woodwork.

Generally, the liquid lead in this range is piped into strips and then applied to the glass when dry. It can be used as normal liquid lead when making peel-off suncatchers. I do find that this type of leading is too thick to be suitable for projects requiring fine-line work, so I do not use it on baubles or anything requiring a lot of detail. The paints can be used with all the other makes of lead.

Piping the lead strips (1)

First, prepare your leading strips. Take a piece of cardboard about 300 x 400mm (12 x 16in), or a small, flat cardboard box, and cover this with a disposable plastic carrier bag. Turn it over, and, using sticky tape, pull this together tightly so that it

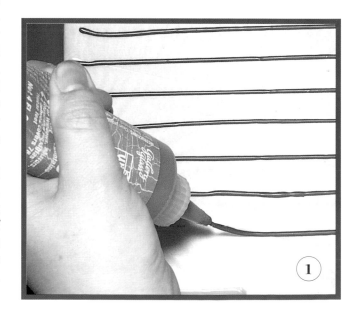

forms a smooth, wrinkle-free surface on the reverse. Stretch-plastic cooking film is not suitable.

Turn the board over, and on this smooth, plastic-covered surface, draw lots of straight parallel lines of lead. Leave these to dry and 'cure'. This will take about twelve hours. When dry, the lines of lead can be lifted from the surface.

Applying the lead strips to the design (2)

Tape your template on to the back of the glass door or window and, using these leaded strips, follow the design of the template. (In the picture I am using a piece of acetate.) The lead will stick to the glass as you press it into place. If the lines of lead meet, cut off the surplus with a craft knife; these 'left-overs' can be used for other smaller areas. When you are fixing the lead into position, it can be lifted and re-applied. Try to avoid excessive handling, as this may affect adhesion.

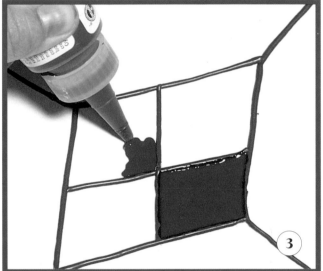

Applying the paint (3)

When you are satisfied with the leading, you can start painting. Apply the glass paint straight from the bottle; the applicator on the end of the bottle makes brushes unnecessary. Just squeeze the bottle and the paint will flow on to the glass. As the paint has a thick texture, it will not run. All colours are intermixable to the surface of the glass.

When applying the colour, as with all glass paints, first apply the colour around the inside edge of the lead before filling in the centre of the section with a generous amount of colour.

Smoothing out the paint (4)

To smooth out the paint and get it to go into all the corners of the outlined area, stir it around with a cocktail stick. Paints appear opaque at first, but will dry transparent in about one to two days, depending on room temperature.

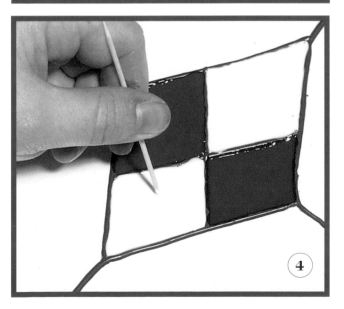

Peel-off suncatchers

Another very interesting way of using the textured paints is to make removable suncatchers. The lead is squeezed directly from the tube on to a smooth surface, not piped and cut; a transparent sheet of acetate is ideal. When dry, they can be peeled off and stuck to any window or mirror without any adhesive, hooks or thread, and they have no frames.

First, test the paint on a spare piece of plastic; this will let you see whether it will allow the suncatcher to be peeled off cleanly and easily.

A selection of peel-off suncatchers made from the textured paint.

See page 76 for the patterns.

Place the design under the plastic sheet and trace it using the special liquid lead. Make sure that all the lines join up leaving enclosed areas into which the paint will be applied. Leave the leading to cure and dry (about twelve hours).

Next, fill in the design with your selected colours. If there is an area in your design that you would like to leave clear, you can use clear texturizing paint (see below). Leave the suncatcher to dry for a further one to two days, then peel it away carefully, in one piece, from the plastic sheet. It can then be stuck on to a window, door or mirror.

Of course, you do not have to make the traditional round suncatcher shape. I make them in many different designs, as you can see here. Be careful not to stick your suncatchers on to painted surfaces, as they may leave a permanent stain.

You can remove suncatchers – perhaps those that have a seasonal design – and store them away for future use: just lift an edge and pull away gently. If the paint seems brittle, warm it gently with a hairdryer. The suncatcher will become pliable and slightly softer, making it much easier to remove.

When not in use, store your suncatcher in a plastic bag. Each one will need a separate bag, as otherwise, they will stick together. Individual sandwich bags are good. Always store them flat.

If, after storage, the suncatchers do not stick when re-applied, try wiping them and the window with window cleaner, and try again.

Clear textured paint

The textured paint range includes a clear transparent paint which is extremely useful and versatile. It is applied, like the coloured paints, directly on to glass or acetate. If you move the nozzle from side to side when applying the paint, it will produce a bumpy, uneven textured finish, not dissimilar to the hand-made glass. It appears milky-white when wet, but dries crystal clear. It is very useful when an obscure finish is needed. Remember that it is water-based and cannot be mixed with solvent-based paints.

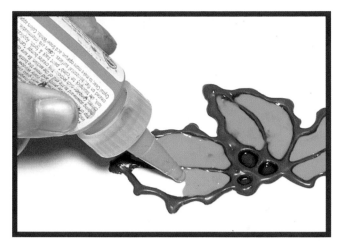

Straight from the tube, the textured paint looks quite milky, but it does dry clear.

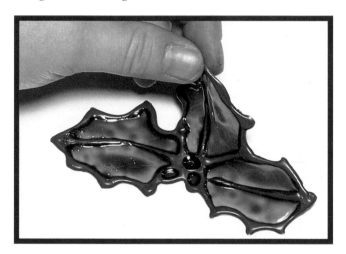

When the design is completely dry, carefully lift it off the plastic and simply apply it to the window.

Detail from dragon painting (see page 30–31) showing the effect of clear textured paint.

Self-adhesive lead strip

This is real lead with an adhesive backing, so it is quite expensive to buy. However, the effect it produces more than justifies the extra cost and effort involved. It is available in different widths, the wider the lead, the more expensive it is. Wide lead is best for fixing panels to existing windows, as it forms a stronger, thicker seal.

I use the narrower lead strip for following templates and patterns, as it is much easier to manipulate. Even this narrow lead can be difficult to bend around corners, so I usually cut it in half with a pair of utility scissors. This has two advantages: first, it makes it really easy to shape and bend round the most intricate patterns; second, you get twice the length of lead, making it twice as economical!

Before you start applying the lead, make sure that the glass or plastic you are using is thoroughly clean and grease-free.

I find it best to leave the leaded design for a day or so, to allow the adhesive to set completely, before sealing (see the instructions on sealing, care and cleaning on page 62). Treat leaded glass as ordinary glass.

I used a combination of self-adhesive lead strip and liquid lead for this panel. The photograph above had light behind it, showing the effect it would produce in daylight. The photograph opposite was taken with a light in front, showing the effect the panel would have against a dark sky in a lighted room.

Image size: 180 x 290mm (7 x 11¹/₂in), on glass.

Stick the self-adhesive lead strip down firmly, using the pressing tool provided with the lead, to form outlined areas which you then paint just as before. It gives a very authentic look, especially if you stick lead on the reverse of the design as well.

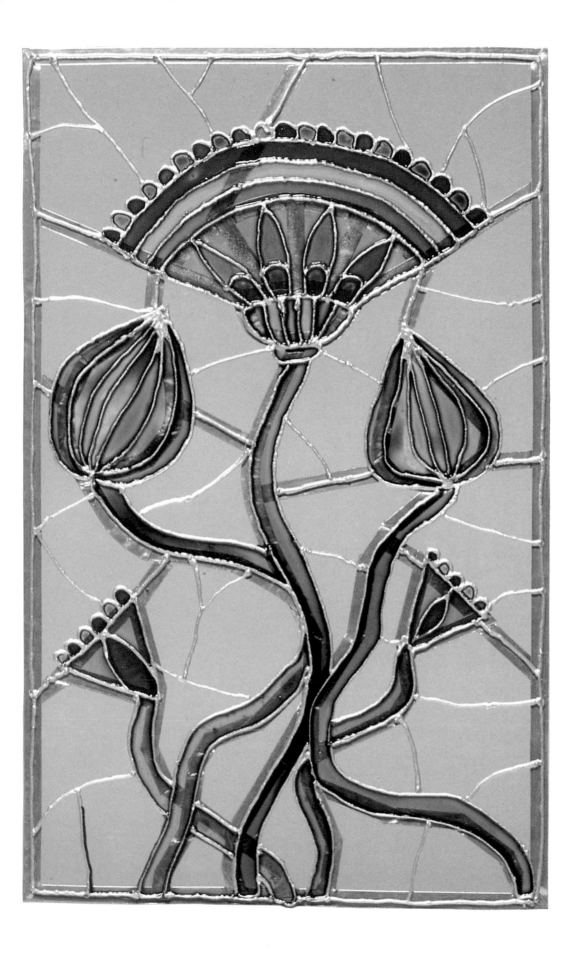

See page 77 for the pattern.

Applying the lead strip

1. Place your design template under a sheet of glass or plastic and secure it in place.

2. Using utility scissors, cut the lead in half along its width. Now plan how you will go about applying the lead. Each piece must to be cut to size; cut the shorter pieces first, remembering to allow for overlaps, followed by the longer pieces.

3. Place each piece of lead into position, gently easing curved pieces into shape without kinking or stretching the lead. Remove the backing strip that covers the adhesive as you work. Gently but firmly press the lead down on to the surface, using the tool supplied with the leading kit, to coax and manipulate the lead around bends. If you are not satisfied with the placing of a lead strip, it can easily be lifted with a craft knife and moved. Try not to touch the adhesive with your hands.

4. When you have applied all the lead, carefully, using the pressing tool, make sure that all the lead is firmly pressed flat to the surface. Pay particular attention to all the joins and overlapping pieces, making sure that they are well sealed together.

5. Remove the paper template and lay the glass down with, the leading on the underside, over a sheet of white paper.

6. Following the lead strip design, trace all the lines using liquid lead. This will contain the areas that will be painted. When the lead has dried, paint the design using solvent-based paint. (See the basic method on pages 12–15.)

7. When it has dried, you can fix the glass panel to an existing window or door. Make sure that the side with the liquid lead and paint is facing away from you, and the side with the lead strip is facing towards you. Fix the panel to the inside of the window in the way explained on page 63.

The photographs (above and opposite) feature my potted primrose painted on glass. For this project, self-adhesive lead strip is applied to one side of the glass and liquid lead and the paint on the other. The painted side is sealed with a coat of varnish to protect it.

Image size: 250 x 300mm (10 x 12in), on glass.

Cut the short pieces to include an overlap.

For a neater appearance, cut the overlapped end at an angle.

Use a pressing tool to make a neat join.

See page 78 for the pattern.

50

Acid-etching effect

An acid-etched effect can be achieved using an acrylic-based medium called frosting varnish. It produces a milky-white opaque finish that has a sanded texture very similar to that of real etched glass. It is easy to use and can be applied vertically.

Before use, the design should be masked with tape on the surface of the glass or plastic (you could also use stencils). The frosting varnish is then painted evenly with a brush, over the area required. While the paint it still wet, go over it with a dry sponge roller. This produces the characteristic rough surface of traditional etching.

However, if you are only intending to produce a small design, there is a faster and easier method. Pour a small amount of the frosting varnish into a saucer, and, using a small sponge, dip this into the varnish and apply to the surface, using a light dabbing movement. I find that this produces the same effect.

When you have finished applying the frosting varnish, carefully remove the masking tape or stencil before the varnish dries, taking care not to smudge any edges. If you do not do this, the varnish may adhere to the tape or stencil. Frosting varnish takes two to four hours to dry.

This example of acid etching is produced on a sheet of acetate. It has been photographed against a dark background to show off the opaque sanded texture.

Paintflow blending

As you have already seen, opaque white paint can be added to the other transparent colours to produce semi-opaque pastels (see the parrot on pages 32–33). But there are lots of other ways that you can use it to produce some very interesting textures and effects.

On the painting of a steam train (opposite), I painted the smoke in white. Then, using the very tip of the brush, I added drops of black and grey to the wet paint. Next, carefully using the tip of the brush, I guided these colours into the thick white paint using short, light strokes. This technique is known as paintflow blending. I find it is also very effective for shading petals on flowers. (The paint effect you can see on the trees is called 'dappling' – see page 55.)

Paintflow blending can also be used to create a marbled texture. First, apply thick white paint to an area, then drop in large blobs of a contrasting colour – vivid or dark colours work best. Now, using a cocktail stick or toothpick, gently swirl the contrasting colour around in the white paint or drag it from side to side to form a layered-line effect.

This technique can be very useful for creating all sorts of textures. You can also reverse this method by painting with transparent colour and then adding the opaque white as a contrast. To get a satisfactory result, however, you must use large amounts of white, as it tends to be overwhelmed by darker colours when used in this way. Try practising this technique on a scrap of acetate to see what effects you can achieve.

53

Image size: 200mm (8in) diameter on glass.

See page 79 for the pattern.

This full-size detail from the picture of the knight (opposite) shows how the dappling technique can be used to good effect on the chain-mail armour. Although most of the leading on the panel is black, I have also used gold leading to highlight certain areas such as the sword and shield.

Image size of the complete panel: 195 x 405mm (7³/₄ x 16in) on glass.

Dappling

This is a painting technique that I find very useful when I want to suggest texture. It involves applying neat white spirit on to a painted surface while the paint is still wet. I have used this effect on the trees in the train painting on page 53, on the Gothic candle-shade on pages 24–25, and on the armour of the knight below and opposite.

1. Slightly dilute a base colour with thinners.

2. Now paint the base colour on to the glass.

3. While this is still wet, take a No. 4 brush and use the very tip to dot the surface of the paint at intervals, using neat white spirit. Each dot will spread slightly into a wider circle, producing interesting effects on the surface of the paint.

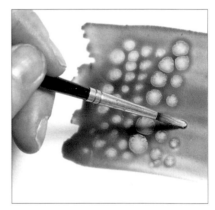

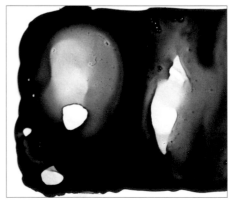

Before working on a real painting, practise your technique on a scrap of glass or acetate, as the results vary widely.

mefa montps et sfpoffend

Shrink plastic

This is a special type of plastic. When you have painted your design on it, you bake it in an oven and it shrinks to about one-third of its original size. It is ideal for small objects with fine details, such as earrings, key-rings and buttons.

You can draw on the plastic using solvent-based felt-tipped pens. (Water-based pens are not suitable as they will not permanently colour the plastic.)

Alternatively, you can use stained-glass paints (water-based or solvent-based). These will produce a rough-textured surface when the plastic has been baked. You can also use liquid lead. As the plastic shrinks, the lead puckers and the lead lines become bunched up. The effect is particularly attractive when gold or silver lead is used. However, use liquid lead sparingly on shrink plastic, as too much can overpower the appearance of the finished piece.

Opposite: A selection of shrink-plastic items. The pendants at the top, and the grape and tulip earrings, were drawn with felt-tipped pens. The others were painted with liquid lead and glass paints. Look at the two sets of tulip earrings to see the different effects.

Below: By way of comparison I have included another collection of pendants which were simply painted on ordinary sheets of acetate.

Drawing your design on the shrink plastic

The shrink-plastic sheets are transparent, so you can trace a design directly on to them. Remember to make your design on the large side to allow for shrinkage. When painting the plastic, you will get better results if you use lighter shades, since colours tend to darken and intensify during baking. When your painting has dried, cut around the edge with scissors. Then, using a punch, make the holes required for earring wires, button holes, etc., as the plastic will be quite thick and rigid after baking.

Baking the shrink plastic

Pre-heat the oven to 180°C (350°F). Place your pieces of shrink plastic on to a cool non-stick baking sheet, spacing them evenly. Place the sheet in the middle of the oven and bake for two to five minutes. If your oven has a glass front, you can check on the pieces while they bake.

Very soon, the pieces will start to curl and distort while they shrink. They will then slowly uncurl, thicken, and lie flat. When this process is complete remove them from the oven, take them off the tray and leave them to cool on a flat surface.

Do experiment – you may need to vary the temperature of your oven to obtain the best results.

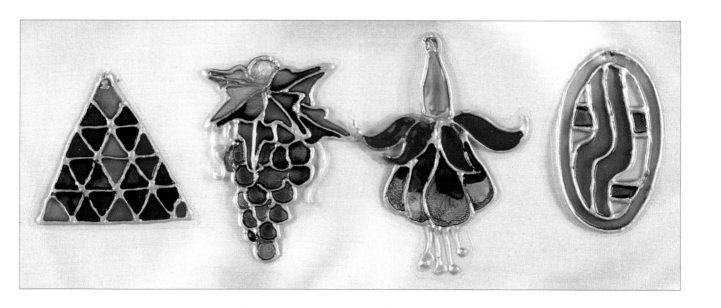

Vat dipping

Vat dipping produces the most astonishing effects in seconds. It can be used on virtually anything transparent, from vases and glasses to jam jars and bottles. However, it can be quite messy, so I always do it outside on a dry day.

You will need
Bucket
Bin-liner (with no holes in it)
Water
Plenty of tissues and rags for cleaning
Solvent-based paints: a few drops of any two or three
  colours you like (you can not use water-based paints
  for this technique.
Thinners

1. Place the bin-liner in the bucket, pulling the edges over the sides, then fill to just over halfway with water.

2. Using the colours of your choice, sprinkle a few drops of each into the water. Do not stir, as this will make the paint disperse to the sides of the bucket. A note of caution: be very sparing if using red, too much will result in a very gruesome and gory appearance!

3. When dipping an object, hold it tightly by the rim, or, if possible, place your hand inside. Then quickly submerge it up to the rim in the water and remove it immediately. The paint will have attached itself to the outside in all sorts of fantastic patterns. Leave on a level surface to dry.

You will only be able to dip, at most, two objects into the paint mixture before it begins to break up in the water. If this happens, try to skim off the remaining paint before adding new. Sometimes, in hot weather, the paint dries on the surface of the water. This will make the paint clot on the object.

When you have finished dipping, remove the bin-liner, (still full of water), from the bucket. Make a few holes in the bottom of the bin-liner, and empty the water down a drain. As the water drains away, the paint will adhere to the sides of the bin-liner. The empty bin-liner can then be thrown away.

Sprinkle a few drops of each colour on to the surface of the water.

Dip the object into the water and pull it out again.

This method, though fun to do, can take a little time to master. If you are not happy with your early efforts, simply wipe the paint from the object (using thinners and a cloth) and try again.

Drawing on dipped items with gold or silver lead

When your dipped items have dried, you can add on gold or silver lead for more decoration. Small, simple designs look best, as too much gold or silver can overwhelm the dipped effect.

Another idea is to follow some of the lines of paint with gold or silver lead for an interesting abstract effect, but again, do not overdo it.

Dipped and leaded items are for decorative use only, but they can be varnished for added protection (see page 62).

A step beyond

Once you have learnt all the techniques in this book and have practised enough, you can go on to do all sorts of other beautiful work, such as these rather more advanced acrylic panels with their more intricate painting and historical style.

The unusual cherub panel (below) was inspired by the classic stained-glass style. The face has been painted using thinned paint and then shaded for a subtle natural look.

The medieval-style angel (opposite) has been made more authentic by the addition of heraldic shields and a scroll with an inscription on it.

Image size: 500mm (20in) square on plastic.

Image size: 410 x 515mm (16¹/₄ x 20¹/₄in) on plastic.

Sealing, care and cleaning

Sealing your painting

Varnishing your finished object will protect it from knocks and scratches which may spoil its painted surface. On flat panels of glass or plastic, apply varnish, liberally but slowly, over the surface using a large flat brush. If you work too quickly air bubbles can appear; these are caused by the friction of the brush as it goes over the raised lines of leaded work, but they should disappear naturally when the varnish has dried.

When sealing jars or bottles, apply one or two coats of varnish. If applied to thickly, the varnish may run while it is drying .

I do not generally bother to varnish mobiles, suncatchers and candle-shades, as I find that these items are rarely scuffed or scratched in use.

Boxes, particularly those with added jewels, should be protected with a liberal coat of varnish. Remember to varnish each side, and let the varnish dry thoroughly before turning the box over to varnish the other sides in turn.

Lead strip can safely be treated as ordinary glass. It needs no varnish for protection.

Care and cleaning

The upkeep of most painted objects is simple:

◆ Occasionally give them a light dusting.

◆ If you want to wash them, always use tepid water and a weak liquid-detergent solution. Wipe over gently and carefully.

◆ Do not rub the painted surface too vigorously, as you may dislodge some of the lead or paint.

◆ Do not leave painted objects to soak in water.

◆ Do not put painted objects in a dishwasher.

◆ You can clean surfaces, and remove fingerprints, with window-cleaning fluid on a soft cloth.

Apply varnish to the painted image only.

Fixing glass panels

Fixing panels with lead strip

Any glass painting can be permanently fixed to an existing window using 9mm ($^3/_8$in) wide, self-adhesive lead strip. For safety, the picture must be painted on lightweight picture glass which is not too thick or heavy. (Other thicknesses of glass may be used when battens are used to fix the panel: see below.) When fixing a picture to an existing window using self-adhesive lead, I recommend that the dimensions of the glass should not exceed 400 x 300mm (16 x 12in).

1. Mark the position of the picture you wish to put on to an existing window with a black china-marking crayon.

2. Turn the picture over, so that the painted side is facing away from you, towards the existing window. Place the panel into position and hold it there temporarily with pieces of strong masking tape. (It is easier if you can get a friend to hold the panel in position while you are working.)

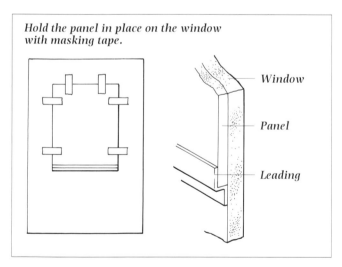

Hold the panel in place on the window with masking tape.

Window

Panel

Leading

3. Having measured each side of the panel, cut strips of self-adhesive lead to size. Slowly and carefully place this along each side of the glass panel,

starting with the lower edge. Remove the masking tape as you go. Using the tool provided with the lead, press the lead firmly into place, making sure that half of the lead's width covers the edge of the glass panel, while the remaining half of the lead width adheres to the existing window behind. Keep pressing and smoothing the lead down to provide a good airtight seal. Pay particular attention to the corners, smoothing down the joins.

Fixing glass panels with wooden battens

Panels to be fitted to existing windows should be the same size as the exposed glass in the window.

Measure the glass and cut the wooden beading to size, with mitred ends. (A timber merchant should be able to do this for you.) Hold the panel in position with the painted side against the glass. Place one piece of batten down one side of the window and secure it to the window frame with panel pins. Repeat with the other three pieces of batten to complete the installation.

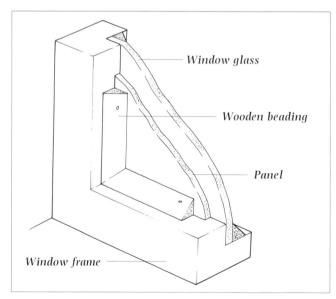

Window glass

Wooden beading

Panel

Window frame

Patterns

See page 8.

See page 17. Note that the
painted version of this design
is viewed from the back.

See page 21.

65

See page 21.

See page 21.

See page 21.

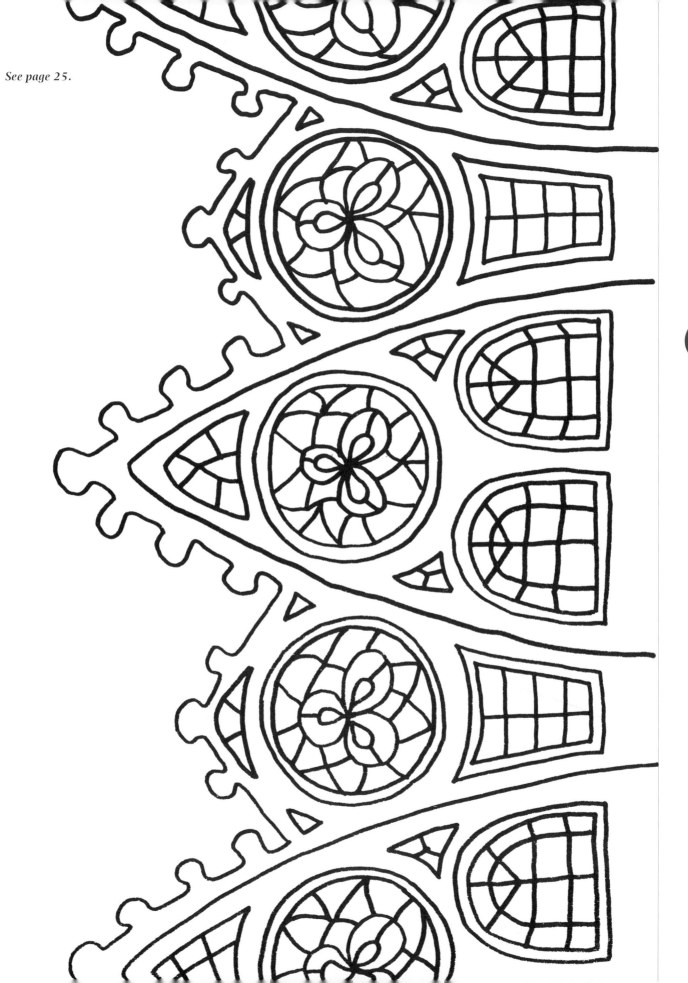

See page 25.

See page 23.

68

See page 29.

See page 26.

See pages 32–33.

See pages 30–31.

See page 36.

See page 41.

See page 46.

See page 46.

See page 47.

See page 46.

See page 44.

See page 49.

See page 51.

See page 53.

Index